CULTURE IN ACTION

Graffiti

Jane Bingham

www.raintreepublishers.co.uk
Visit our website to find out more information about Raintree books.

To order:
☎ Phone +44 (0) 1865 888066
🗎 Fax +44 (0) 1865 314091
🖳 Visit www.raintreepublishers.co.uk

Raintree is an imprint of Capstone Global Library Limited, a company incorporated in England and Wales having its registered office at 7 Pilgrim Street, London, EC4V 6LB – Registered company number: 6695582

"Raintree" is a registered trademark of Pearson Education Limited, under licence to Capstone Global Library Limited

Text © Capstone Global Library Limited 2010
First published in hardback in 2010

Edited by Louise Galpine, Rachel Howells, and Helen Cox
Designed by Kimberly Miracle and Betsy Wernert
Original illustrations © Capstone Global Library Ltd.
Illustrated by kja-artists.com
Picture research by Mica Brancic and Kay Altwegg
Production by Alison Parsons
Originated by Steve Walker, Capstone Global Library Ltd
Printed in China by Leo Paper Products Ltd

ISBN 978 1 406212 07 5 (hardback)
14 13 12 11 10
10 9 8 7 6 5 4 3 2 1

British Library Cataloguing in Publication Data
Bingham, Jane
Graffiti. – (Culture in action)
751.7'3
A full catalogue record for this book is available from the British Library.

Acknowledgements

We would like to thank the following for permission to reproduce photographs: Alamy pp. **6** (Eddie Gerald), **7 bottom** (Tony Watson), **8** (© David Wheeldon), **15** (Tony Lilley), **19** (Darrin Jenkins), **20** (Stock Italia), **25** (Michael Klinec), **26** (EuroStyle Graphics); Corbis p. **16** (Adam Woolfitt); Corbis SYGMA p. **18** (Julio Donoso); Getty Images pp. **5** (Paul Hawthorne), **17 bottom** (AFP/Aris Messinis), **22** (AFP/Timothy A. Clary), **27** (Scott Barbour); iStockphoto **14** (© Michael Valdez), **17 top** (Terraxplorer); Photofusion pp. **12** (Janine Wiedel), **24** (© Colin Edwards); Shutterstock pp. **4** (© Sam Cornwell), **7 top** (© Dubassy), **9** (© Stuart Weston), **11** (© Tyler Boyes).

Icon and banner images supplied by Shutterstock: © Alexander Lukin, © ornitopter, © Colorlife, and © David S. Rose.

Cover photograph of student volunteers painting legal graffiti in preparation for the 2008 Olympics in Beijing, China, reproduced with permission of Corbis (epa/Michael Reynolds).

We would like to thank Susie Hodge, Jackie Murphy, and Nancy Harris for their invaluable help in the preparation of this book.

Every effort has been made to contact copyright holders of material reproduced in this book. Any omissions will be rectified in subsequent printings if notice is given to the publishers.

Contents

What is graffiti?   4

Why create graffiti?   6

Types and styles   8

A very long history   14

Graffiti, art, and music   18

The problem of graffiti   24

What next?   26

Timeline   28

Glossary   30

Find out more   31

Index   32

Important note:

It is fine to draw "graffiti style" designs on paper, or in special places where you have permission. But you should NEVER paint or draw on other people's property without permission.

Some words are printed in bold, **like this**. You can find out what they mean by looking in the glossary on page 30.

What is graffiti?

Graffiti is the name given to writing, designs, or pictures on walls or other surfaces. It is often done without permission, although there are some places where graffiti is allowed.

Even though writing on public and private property is against the **law**, people still do it. People have been creating graffiti for thousands of years.

An ancient name

The word *graffiti* comes from the Greek word for "writing". People who paint graffiti in the streets are usually known as "graffiti writers".

Sometimes, a run-down city street can become covered by graffiti.

Scratches and spray paint

Graffiti comes in several different forms. Sometimes people scratch initials, words, or designs onto a surface. Often graffiti is painted, using a paintbrush or a can of spray paint.

Today, most graffiti writers use spray paints to create colourful effects. Spray paints can be used to create freehand designs or to make **stencils** (see page 19). Some graffiti writers use thick marker pens to achieve speedy results.

Art or crime?

Many people see graffiti as a crime. They claim it destroys the environment of our towns and cities. Others think graffiti can look good, and even see it as a form of art. What do you think about graffiti?

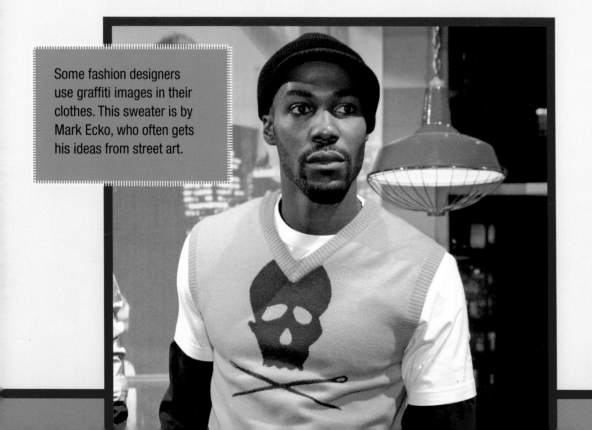

Some fashion designers use graffiti images in their clothes. This sweater is by Mark Ecko, who often gets his ideas from street art.

Why create graffiti?

What is it that makes someone write on walls and other surfaces? There are several reasons why people decide to make their mark on their environment.

I was here

Graffiti is a way of showing that you have been in a certain place. Prisoners locked in dungeons, pupils sitting at a desk, and tourists visiting a distant monument have all felt the urge to leave some evidence that they were there.

In the past, people simply wrote their name. Often the name was shortened to initials (which are quicker and easier to carve or write). Sometimes they added the date as well. Today, most graffiti writers use a short nickname, known as a **tag**.

Painting the Berlin Wall

From 1961 to 1989, the city of Berlin was divided by a famous wall. On one side was West Berlin and on the other was East Berlin. East Berlin was part of East Germany, a **communist** society where everyone was meant to be equal. Nobody was allowed to cross the wall, but people in the west protested by covering the wall with graffiti.

This section of the Berlin Wall is now on display in London.

A tag shows that the graffiti writer has visited a place. Writers try to get their tags in as many places as possible.

Something to say

Some people use graffiti to express their views. Writing a message in a public place is a way of stating your point of view. This kind of graffiti is meant to be easily seen. It is usually painted in large capital letters.

This graffiti piece is by the British artist Banksy. It makes the point that everyone is watched by closed circuit television cameras.

Types and styles

Today's graffiti writers use a range of styles. Some simple graffiti can be done very quickly. Other pieces have a lot of pattern and colour and take many hours to complete.

Tags

The most basic element in graffiti is the **tag**. In its simplest form, it is a kind of signature, done in spray paint or marker pen. Having a tag helps **illegal** writers to avoid punishment. When they use a tag, their real name can remain unknown.

Throw-ups

When graffiti writers want to paint a bolder version of their tag, they create a "throw-up". These strong designs are quick and easy to "throw up" on a wall. Writers first paint the letter outlines of their tag. Then they fill in the outlines with a different coloured paint. Most throw-ups use two strongly contrasting colours, such as red and blue, or silver and black.

Throw-ups are sometimes known as "fill-ins" or "dubs". Dubs is short for "double colours".

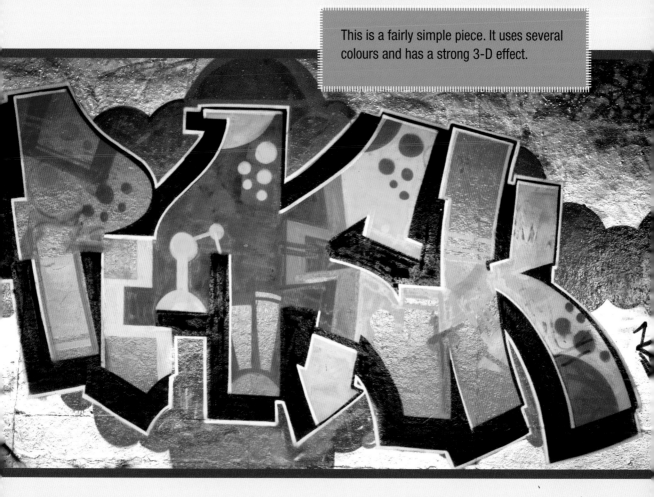

This is a fairly simple piece. It uses several colours and has a strong 3-D effect.

Pieces

A piece is an elaborate version of the artist's tag. The word "piece" comes from "masterpiece". The letters in a piece are first outlined and then filled in, using three or more colours. Pieces use fancy lettering styles (see pages 10–11). They often include **3-D** effects so the letters seem to stand out from the wall.

Penguin graffiti

A graffiti artist called Banksy once painted a message at London Zoo. He climbed into the penguin **enclosure** and wrote in very large letters: "We're bored of fish."

Straights

The simplest letters used in graffiti are block capitals, also known as **straights**. Straights are usually painted in just two colours, for the outline and the fill-in. Occasionally, a third colour is added to give a 3-D effect.

Bubbles

Bubble letters are rounded versions of ordinary letters. They have curvy outlines so that they can fit snugly into each other. Because bubble letters are so wide, they provide a great surface for **colour fades** (two colours merged gradually into each other).

Write your name in bubble letters

First write your name in capital letters. Then draw around each letter to create bubble letters. Make each letter overlap the one behind. When you are happy with your name, erase the first marks you made and give the letters a two-colour fade and a strong black outline.

Wildstyle

Wildstyle lettering is the hardest to create. The letters have sharp outlines and they all fit very tightly together, like a complicated jigsaw puzzle. Wildstyle pieces often feature arrows pointing in different directions. They are intended to be works of art, rather than words that are easy to read.

Characters

Some graffiti pieces include a cartoon character, either inside the letters or beside the piece. Graffiti writers create their own characters, but cartoon monsters and aliens are very popular.

In a wildstyle piece, all the letters fit together to create a total design.

The wall of this youth centre has a graffiti production on the subject of sport.

Productions

Some graffiti writers create large-scale **murals**, called productions. Productions combine several pieces and characters. They are often made by a group of writers working together.

Productions usually have a single-colour background. They often have a theme, such as "under the sea" or "out in space".

Animal tags

Graffiti writers often choose a tag that shows something about them. Can you think of an animal tag that reflects your personality? Are you a tiger, a turtle, or a rhino? When you have decided on your animal, you are ready to create your tag.

Steps to follow:

1. Practise writing your animal tag in graffiti style. (It helps if your name is not too long!) You can use bubble letters or straights.

2. Choose two or more colours for your tag. Practise using your colours for outlines, fill-ins, and colour fades.

3. When you are happy with your tag, draw a small cartoon character of your animal. It can be a face or a whole animal, but keep it really simple.

4. Now put your tag and your character together, and stand back and admire your piece!

You can also combine several pieces and characters to make a production. Your production will have an animal theme.

A very long history

When did graffiti begin? Some people claim that **prehistoric** rock art is the earliest form of graffiti. They give examples of cave paintings dating back 30,000 years. Other people think that graffiti began soon after humans learned to write, around 5,000 years ago. But, whenever it started, graffiti has a very long history.

Ancient writings

Messages and names have been found on the walls of buildings from ancient Egypt, Greece, and Rome. In North America, carvings survive on the stones of Mayan temples in Mexico, dating from around 400 BCE. That is around 2,400 years ago.

This ancient graffiti was found in rocks in the Nevada Desert, USA. It dates from around 10,000 years ago.

These examples of Roman graffiti were found in the buried city of Pompeii, Italy. They have survived for almost 2,000 years.

Roman records

The best examples of early graffiti come from the Roman city of Pompeii in Italy. In 79 CE (around 1,900 years ago), Pompeii was completely buried in ash, when a nearby volcano erupted. Hundreds of years later, **archaeologists** (people who learn about the past) uncovered the city. They found many walls carved with Roman graffiti.

The people of Pompeii carved messages of love, curses on their enemies, and magic spells. The Roman graffiti included quotes from famous writers and cartoon drawings of local **politicians**.

Stupid scribblers

"I wonder, O wall, that you have not fallen in ruins from supporting the stupidities of so many scribblers."

Roman graffiti on a wall in Pompeii.

Medieval marks

Many examples of graffiti have survived from the **medieval** (1000–1450 CE) period. Prisoners in dungeons scratched their names and the dates they were there. Some even wrote last messages before they died. Medieval builders carved special signs, known as masons' marks, into the beams and walls of buildings where they were working.

Travellers and soldiers

By the 1800s, tourists and travellers were carving their names on monuments in distant places. There are also examples of graffiti by soldiers. Many young men left a record of their names before they went into battle.

Sign that rock!

In the 1840s, many people travelled west across America in the hope of finding gold. This race to find riches was called the gold rush. Some people carved their names on the rocks they passed. One boulder in Wyoming is called the Signature Rock because it has so many names carved into it.

The graffiti writers of the 1960s started a trend for writing on trains. This is a subway in New York City, USA.

Spray-paint graffiti

In the 1960s, some people in New York City, USA, began using spray paint to create graffiti. They painted **tags** in public places, and especially on **subway** trains. Some of them created complete spray-art scenes on long stretches of tunnels and walls.

The new graffiti style spread rapidly. Today you can see examples of spray-can graffiti in most cities of the world.

Some of the names carved into this Greek temple date back to the 1890s. Carving on ancient monuments like this is actually a crime.

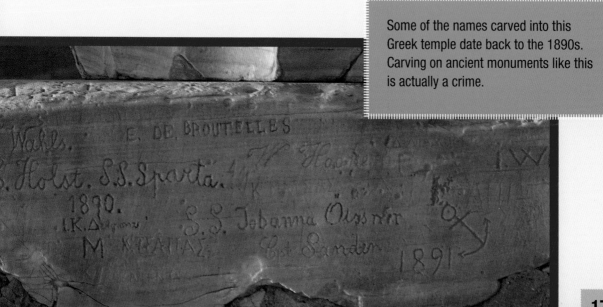

Graffiti, art, and music

Graffiti has become part of modern **culture**. It has strong links with **hip hop** and **rap** music. Many modern artists use graffiti styles in their paintings. Designers create fashions that are strongly influenced by street art. There are even computer games about graffiti.

From the street to the gallery

In the 1980s, some graffiti writers began to paint on **canvases** as well as in the streets. Jean-Michel Basquiat and Keith Haring both started out as graffiti artists in New York City. Later, they became leading figures in the art world. Today, many graffiti artists create canvases for galleries.

Basquiat's works on canvas kept many elements of graffiti style.

Banksy

One of the best-known graffiti artists is Banksy. He is based in the UK, but he has also painted in Australia and the United States.

Banksy uses **stencil** designs to create very striking images. His art can be funny but it often has a serious aim. Some of his paintings ask difficult questions, such as what is the point of war?

Banksy created this stencil in Camden, North London, in 2006.

Keith Haring

Keith Haring was influenced by graffiti and comic art. When he was an art student he began to draw simple chalk figures in the New York City **subway**. Later, he created **murals**, paintings, and sculptures. They all feature colourful figures.

Keith Haring's figures are easy to recognize. They have large, circular heads and they are surrounded by lots of short lines. The lines help to express the figures' feelings, like **expression lines** in comics.

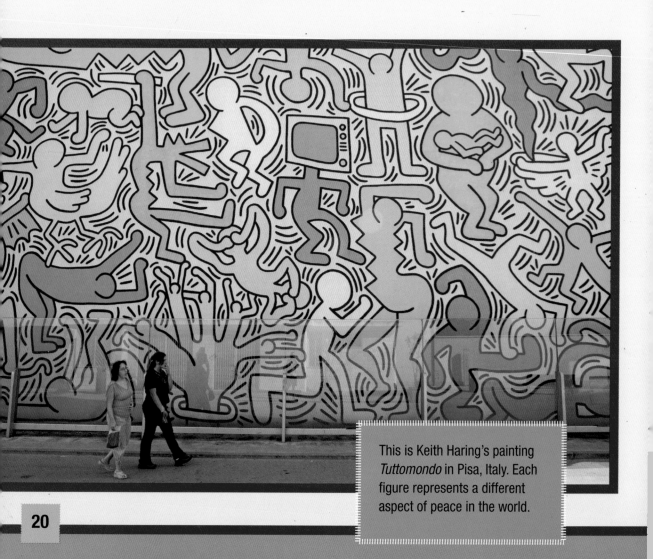

This is Keith Haring's painting *Tuttomondo* in Pisa, Italy. Each figure represents a different aspect of peace in the world.

Figures with feeling

Keith Haring's figures show different emotions through their body shapes. Try using your body to show an emotion. You can work in pairs or in larger groups.

Steps to follow:

1. Use your body to **mime** some emotions. Remember a moment when you felt angry or sad, and try to show your feelings through your actions. Make an effort to use all the parts of your body.

2. Choose the emotion you are happiest with. Mime the emotion and then freeze like a statue. Get your partner (or the rest of the group) to guess what emotion you are showing.

3. Decide on some good body shapes. Then draw their outlines on a large piece of paper. Work in pairs, taking it in turns to be the person miming the emotion, and the one drawing their partner's body shape. Make your figures very simple.

4. Paint your figures in bright colours. Cut them out and stick them on to an even larger strip of paper to make a mural. Add expression lines to help show the figures' feelings.

The DJ Grandmaster Flash was an important figure in the early years of hip hop, when graffiti, music, and dance all developed together.

Graffiti and hip hop

Spray-can graffiti, **breakdancing**, and hip-hop music began in New York City in the 1960s. At that time, graffiti writers and rap artists were often members of the same group of friends.

Today, there is still a very strong link between hip hop and graffiti. Graffiti is one of the four elements of hip-hop culture. The other three elements are: rapping, **DJing** (presenting records), and breakdancing. (Look at the hip-hop book in this series to find out more about the elements of hip hop.)

Signature tune

Graffiti writers use shapes and colours to create their **tags** or signatures. But have you ever tried to create a signature in sound? In this activity you make up your own signature tune. Then you turn it into a rap.

Steps to follow:

1. First think of a short way to introduce yourself. For example, "I am Abby and I love to dance." Or "Omar's my name and chess is my game!" Clap the rhythm with your hands as you say the words.

2. When you are happy with your introduction, try turning it into a very short rap. The rap should say something about you. It's fun if it rhymes, but it doesn't have to.

3. Try to keep up the rhythm of your rap, by clapping your hands or tapping your feet. You could add some dance actions, too.

You could rap together in a group, each taking turns to perform your signature tune.

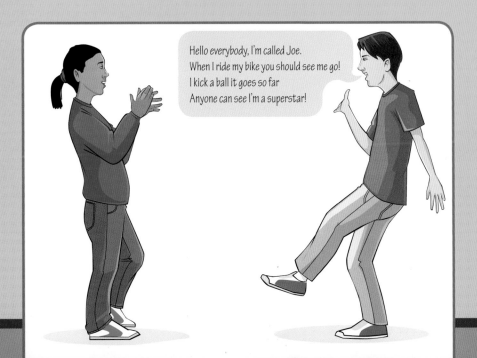

Hello everybody, I'm called Joe.
When I ride my bike you should see me go!
I kick a ball it goes so far
Anyone can see I'm a superstar!

The problem of graffiti

Skilful graffiti on legal walls can look great. But when a building is plastered with **tags**, it can look ugly, messy, and depressing. Careless graffiti can ruin the look of homes, shops, and restaurants. It can cause permanent damage to old and beautiful buildings. It can also be extremely expensive to clean up.

It is not surprising that many people think that graffiti should be banned. But what is being done to stop it?

Graffiti and crime?

Some people claim that graffiti encourages crime. They believe that once an area is covered with graffiti, people stop looking after it. Other damage follows, such as broken windows, and soon there are break-ins and thefts. However, not everyone believes that graffiti leads to crime. Some people think that legal graffiti can improve an **urban** environment.

Messy graffiti like this makes an area look ugly and rundown.

24

It's a crime

In most countries, writing graffiti without permission is a crime. People who are caught painting on walls can be given large fines. If they have caused serious damage they can go to prison for up to 10 years. However, it isn't easy to find the people who do it. **Illegal** graffiti writers can be very hard to track down.

Cleaning up

Most city authorities try to stop graffiti. They run regular clean-up programmes and paint buildings with anti-graffiti paint. Often, graffiti writers who have been caught are made to join a clean-up team.

Here, a worker is using special chemicals to get rid of graffiti from the side of a train.

What next?

Will street art still be fashionable in 10 years' time? Or will graffiti writers be driven off the streets? Nobody knows what will happen to graffiti, but a few new trends have emerged.

Walls of fame

Some authorities have created spaces where graffiti writers can work legally. These legal walls are sometimes known as "walls of fame" because they give artists a chance to show their work.

Many people hope that legal walls will help to solve the graffiti problem. If artists have good spaces where they can express themselves, they may not feel the need to paint **illegally**.

This is part of a wall of fame at Venice Beach, California.

In many places, graffiti has become part of the everyday **urban** environment.

Woodblock graffiti

In the last few years, some graffiti writers have started painting on wood. They paint on plywood boards, which they attach to street signs with metal bolts. This type of street art is known as woodblock graffiti. It displays the writer's skill without damaging buildings or walls.

Clean stencils

Recently, there has been a trend for a new kind of **stencil** graffiti. Artists tape a stencil to a very dirty wall. Then they spray it with a strong cleaning fluid, leaving a clean design on the wall. The only way to remove the stencil is to clean the whole wall!

Timeline

c. 60,000	Humans start painting on cave walls.
c. 3300	Picture writing is invented in the Middle East.
c. 3100	Egyptian builders carve graffiti in stone quarries.
c. 3000	The first carvings are made on Graffiti Rock in Saudi Arabia.
c. 1100	The Greeks carve graffiti on their monuments.
c. 750	Roman towns and cities have many examples of carved graffiti.

CE

c. 200	Mayans carve graffiti in the city of Tikal in Mexico.
c. 790	Vikings from Scandinavia begin their raids on Europe. They leave examples of carved graffiti.
c. 800	European builders and soldiers carve graffiti on castle and cathedral walls.
c. 1350	Italian artists carve their names on ancient Roman monuments.
c. 1554	Lord Guilford Dudley probably carves "Jane" in the Tower of London while he waits to be executed. Jane was the name of his wife, Lady Jane Grey.
c. 1800	Tourism starts to become popular. Early tourists carve their names on monuments.
1818	Giovanni Belzoni carves his name and the date on a pyramid he discovers in Egypt.
1848	The American gold rush begins. People carve their names on rocks on the way to California.

1914	World War I begins in Europe and lasts until 1918. Soldiers leave carved records of their names.
1939	World War II begins in Europe and lasts until 1945. American soldiers leave carved and painted graffiti in Europe and the Far East.
1949	American inventor Edward Seymour invents canned spray paint.
1960s	Rival gangs in U.S. cities start painting **tags**. **Hip hop** begins in New York City, USA.
1970s	Graffiti writers in New York City use spray cans to paint **subway** trains, tunnels, and walls.
1977	Jean-Michel Basquiat starts painting graffiti in New York City.
1980	Keith Haring starts making chalk drawings in the New York City subway.
1981	Graffiti artist Blek le Rat starts creating **stencils** in Paris, France.
1982	New York City **Rap** Tour visits Paris and London, introducing graffiti and rap to Europe.
1989	The Clean Train Movement begins in New York City. It is one of many campaigns to remove and prevent graffiti.
1992	Banksy starts to paint his stencils.
2008	An exhibition of pieces by Banksy and other stencil artists is held in a disused railway tunnel in London.

Glossary

3-D three dimensional. A 3-D shape has three dimensions (length, width, and depth).

archaeologist someone who learns about the past by uncovering and studying old buildings and objects

breakdancing very energetic and acrobatic dancing, involving lots of moves close to the ground

canvas surface used for painting, made from heavy cloth stretched over a wooden frame

colour fade colour that slowly fades and changes into another colour

communist system of organizing a country so that all the land, houses, and factories belong to the state and all the profits are shared by everyone

culture ways that people express themselves through art, music, dance, writing, and theatre

DJing presenting records by mixing and scratching

enclosure place where animals are kept

expression line line that artists use to show feelings

hip hop culture that began in New York City in the 1960s

illegal against the law

law rules of a country, set by the government. It is against the law to use graffiti in many places, but in some places it is allowed.

medieval belonging to a period of history between around 1000 and 1450

mime act using movements and actions instead of words

mural wall painting

politician someone involved in governing a country

prehistoric belonging to a time very long ago before history was written down

rap talking with a background of music, using rhythm and rhyme

stencil paintings made by spraying paint on a card with a shape cut out of it

straights simple capital letters

subway tunnel where underground trains run

tags short nicknames used by graffiti writers

urban belonging to towns and cities

Find out more

Books

Culture in Action: Hip Hop, Jim Mack (Capstone, 2009)

Graffiti Coloring Book, Uzi (Dokument, 2009)

Websites

http://kids.tate.org.uk/games/street-art
An interactive website from the Tate Modern art gallery, which gives you the chance to create your own graffiti on screen.

www.haringkids.com
This brilliant website is based on the art of Keith Haring, and has lots of activities.

www.artofthestate.co.uk/banksy/banksy.htm
This website has over 300 examples of Banksy's pieces.

Places to see graffiti

The places listed below are either legal walls or places where you can see the work of famous graffiti artists.

London
South Bank skate park (near Waterloo Bridge): a popular legal graffiti site.

Victoria Embankment (close to Temple Underground Station): two Banksy stencils featuring a rat.

Bristol
Stokes Croft: a large Banksy stencil called "The Mild Mild West".

United States: New York City
East Harlem Graffiti Wall of Fame, 106th Street and Park Avenue: a world-famous graffiti site that was started in the 1980s and is still being added to today.

Australia: Sydney
Sydney University Graffiti Tunnel: a famous Australian legal wall.

Index

3-D effects 9, 10

ancient graffiti 14–15
anti-graffiti paint 25

Banksy 7, 9, 10, 19
Basquiat, Jean-Michel 18
Berlin Wall 6
breakdancing 22
bubble letters 10
builders 16

canvas, working on 18
capital letters 7, 10
careless graffiti 24
cartoon characters 11
cave paintings 14
cleaning up graffiti 24, 25
colours 8, 9, 10
    backgrounds 12
    colour fades 10
computer games 18
contemporary artists 18
crime 4, 5, 17, 24, 25

dates 6
DJing 22
dubs 8

Ecko, Mark 5
emotions 20, 21
expression lines 20

fashion design 5, 18
fill-ins 8
freehand designs 5

gold rush 16
graffiti
    history of 14–17
    music, links with 18, 22
    on canvas 18
    reasons for 6–7
    types and styles 8–13
graffiti writers 4, 12, 18,
        25, 26
    working in groups 12
Grandmaster Flash 22

Haring, Keith 18, 20, 21
hip hop 18, 22

initials 5, 6

law 4
legal walls 26
lettering styles 9, 10–11

marker pens 5, 8
masons' marks 16
Mayan temples 14
medieval graffiti 16
murals 12, 20

New York City 17, 22
painting 5
    spray paints 5, 8, 17
pieces 9
points of view, expressing 7
Pompeii 15
prehistoric rock art 14
prisoners 6, 16
productions 12, 13

rap 18, 22, 23
Roman graffiti 15

schoolchildren 6
scratches 5
Signature Rock, Wyoming 16
signatures 6, 8
signature tunes 23
soldiers 16
spray paints 5, 8, 17
stencils 5, 19, 27
straights 10
street art 5, 18, 26
subways 17, 20

tags 6, 7, 8, 9, 17, 23, 24
    animal tags 13
    pieces 9
    throw-ups 8
temples 14, 17
throw-ups 8
tourists 6, 16

urban environments 24

walls of fame 26
wildstyle lettering 11
woodblock graffiti 27